INTRODUCTION

Twenty years ago there were American Pit Bull Terriers, American Staffordshire Terriers, and Staffordshire Bull Terriers along with a wide variety of other Bulldog, Bull Terrier, and mastiff-type breeds. Experienced dog people knew each breed by name and could easily distinguish one from another. The dog-owning pet population could have cared less unless they were fortunate enough to have one of these breeds share their heart and hearth.

Today, experienced dog people can still tell the difference, but the rest of the world reacts in terror to two little words that have come to encompass a surprisingly large number of breeds—the dreaded "pit bull!"

While, technically, the generic "pit bull" does not exist as a specific breed, media horror stories have caused the public at large to consider breeds from the powerful American Pit Bull Terrier to the cute wrinkly Chinese Shar-Pei to be inherently dangerous to themselves and their children. To meet this perceived threat, a multitude of well-meaning but misguided legislation has been enacted not only in the United States but also throughout the world.

The primary danger posed by existing and future breed-specific legislation is the inability of those with the authority to do so to properly identify the breed or breeds in question. Further, the fact that some dogs have caused injuries should not in itself condemn entire breeds of dogs to severe control or possible extinction. This is why the primary thrust of dog organizations and other interested groups has been directed toward generalized, non-breed specific vicious dog laws.

The American Pit Bull Terrier is often feared as an overly aggressive dog and has become the most maligned canine in modern times because of two simple words — "pit bull."

Unfortunately even then, many dogs are unfairly targeted when well-meaning public officials attempt to punish the offending canine and his owner.

Amidst this mess, and there is really no other way to describe the current situation, sits one breed in particular that has become the most maligned canine in modern times merely because the breed's name contains those two dreaded words-"pit bull."

HISTORY OF THE PIT BULL

To understand the American Pit Bull Terrier and how he has come to be perceived, one must first look at the original development of the breed. Ancient dogs, the first animals domesticated by man, were not neatly divided into the different breeds we have today. Rather, they existed in very generalized groups of canines based upon the work they performed. Over time, the most desirable traits of each individual dog were preserved and refined by selective breeding. Thus it took many years before more distinct categories of dogs began to appear, and even then, the dogs were classified primarily according to function. The first three groups of related dog types included the large, smooth-coated mastiff type, the large, heavy-coated flock guardians, and the medium-sized, smooth-coated dogs that were bred for bull and bear baiting.

It was these medium-sized, smooth-coated dogs that eventually developed into the Bulldog and the Boxer. The Bulldog, unlike the overdone specimens we have today, was once a very agile, athletic dog. He had a strong, well-muscled body and a fearless temperament.

Sharing the qualities of the bull and bear baiters of the past, today's Pit Bulls are strong, well-muscled, and fearless.

Early in the American history of the Pit Bull, the breed proved effective in agricultural settings. They were primarily used for guarding homes and flocks and controlling predators.

These dogs became quite popular with the working class because of their outstanding abilities in bull and bear baiting. Prior to the British Humane Act of 1835, blood sports were legal and attracted much interest and considerable wagering from working men and members of royalty alike.

While bull and bear baiting were the most popular sports, minimal interest was paid to dog fighting. However, following the British Humane Act, dog fighting became much more popular as it required minimal space and could be conducted in out of the way locations. As interest in dog fighting increased, the matches became more organized with rules of combat and formal conditioning programs designed to optimize the natural abilities of the dogs. This also led to concerted efforts to breed faster and fiercer fighters by introducing terrier stock into the bloodlines. The results of these crosses were commonly referred to as "bull and terriers." They were so successful that continued breeding led to further development of a more specific breed type.

At the same time, blood sports were also popular in America, and British dogs were regularly imported for this purpose.

Dog fighting was a very popular sport, even more so after the British Humane Act of 1835 that made it illegal. It then took to the back streets.

Although some would disagree, the American Pit Bull Terrier (left) and the American Staffordshire Terrier (right) are very similar and in 1936 were considered the same breed.

American breeding programs followed similar lines as those in Britain, but being in a larger area with a primarily agricultural economy, the dogs proved effective for other purposes. Primary among these were guarding the homestead, protecting the flocks, and controlling predators. This led to breeding for greater size and weight.

While the pioneer settler could have cared less about the lineage of his dogs, the dog fighter kept highly detailed records. It was from these pedigrees that the breed would eventually be registered with one or more kennel clubs.

In the late 1900s, Mr. C.Z. Bennett petitioned the American Kennel Club for registration privileges for his dogs. Frustrated by their continued refusal to grant

The American Pit Bull Terrier became the first breed registered with the United Kennel Club, which was founded by C. Z. Bennett in 1898 because the American Kennel Club kept rejecting his Pit Bulls for registration.

Although still a puppy, this American Pit Bull Terrier will grow to become a powerful, well-muscled dog like so many of his ancestors.

access to their stud book, Mr. Bennett founded the United Kennel Club in 1898 for the sole purpose of registering what would eventually be known as the American Pit Bull Terrier. The breed was known by many names throughout its history, including the Pit Bulldog, American Bull Terrier, and Yankee Terrier. In 1909, the American Dog Breeders Association was formed and also accepted the American Pit Bull Terrier into its registry. Finally, in 1936, the American Kennel Club accepted the breed as the Staffordshire Terrier. The name was later revised to the American Staffordshire Terrier, effective January 1, 1972. This change was necessary to differentiate the American breed from the Staffordshire Bull Terrier (well known in England).

Though American Staffordshire Terrier fanciers would have you believe that their breed and the American Pit Bull Terrier are separate and distinct breeds, that is not the case. They were the same dogs in 1936 and, as evidenced by the dual American Kennel Club and United Kennel Club registrations of many individual dogs, are still very similar today. Of the three registries, the one showing the most disparity is the American Dog Breeders Association, whose members prefer a leaner and much gamer dog than either of the other registries.

However, regardless of the registry, these dogs were all bred for their stability of temperament with humans. While some may find it surprising, even the fighting dogs had to have the stability to be handled by people in and out of the sports arena. No one wanted a dog that would accidentally attack a person. Then why, one would ask, have there been so many vicious attacks credited to the breed?

First of all, it is unknown how many attacks were actually made by American Pit Bull Terriers. So many other breeds have been identified by the catch-all phrase "pit bull" that it is almost impossible to verify which, if any, registered dogs were involved. Further, media information as well as official reports rarely provide sufficient information as to the circumstances surrounding the incident. The breed is fiercely loyal and will guard its master and home when necessary. Thus, many of these incidents may have been provoked. Others may have been initiated by owners who have trained their dogs to be man-aggressive. It is not characteristic of the breed to bite indiscriminately. Unfortunately, when an attack does occur, the damage that an American Pit Bull Terrier can inflict is often severe, which has led to the media outcry against the breed. However, the breed that consistently ranks number one among breeds reported to have been involved in bite incidents, namely the Cocker Spaniel, has not received a fraction of the notoriety.

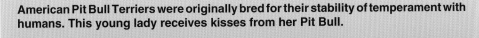

American Pit Bull Terriers were originally bred for their stability of temperament with humans. This young lady receives kisses from her Pit Bull.

Knowing his role as protector of home and family, Tuff to Beat, owned by Eugene Mikell, sits in front of the doorway to discourage any unwelcome guests.

BREED CHARACTERISTICS

While the purpose for which he was originally bred has long since become illegal, the American Pit Bull Terrier remains a functional canine. He has proven to be highly versatile and he can easily redirect his high energy, great strength, and keen intelligence into a variety of activities. Many coupled with another tracking breed that will trail the prey until the hunters are ready to move in for the kill. The American Pit Bull Terrier is then used to "catch and hold" the prey so that the animal can neither get away from the hunters nor charge at and injure them.

The American Pit Bull Terrier has an uncanny ability to distinguish friend from foe, and obviously this youngster is a good friend.

have excelled in obedience, agility, and weight pulling events. They enjoy therapy work and related training. Generally, the breed is extremely willing to please and is easily trained with a firm but loving hand.

Further, the American Pit Bull Terrier and his kin have proved skillful and tenacious in large game hunting. They are usually

The American Pit Bull Terrier has also proven to be a consummate protector of the home and family. He is extremely loyal and enjoys the company of people. He will eagerly greet friends with much tail wagging. However, once taught good judgment, the dog will steadfastly stop an intruder or someone perceived as threatening.

Skillful, tenacious, and hard working, this American Pit Bull Terriers expends some extra energy on the springpole.

American Pit Bull Terriers have the uncanny ability to distinguish friend from foe. They are natural guardians without the need for specialized protection training, though many have excelled at Schutzhund and French Ring Sport. They bond closely with their owners and will read situations from the reactions of their family members as well as those of outside individuals. In the event that a person that the dog has never met but the owner is comfortable with comes to the door, the dog will greet him as a friend. Should the owner be slightly uncomfortable with the situation, the dog will place himself between the owner and the stranger just in case something unfavorable should occur. In the face of a direct threat, the dog will react immediately and appropriately. This is characteristic of a dog that is sound in both mind and body.

Outside the home, the American Pit Bull Terrier is eye catching, sociable, and often draws a crowd. It is interesting to note how many people will rush up and pet the dog, who will respond enthusiastically to the attention. While asking what kind of dog he has just gotten up close and personal with, the same person will often jump back in horror when he is told the name of the breed. The dog has not changed one iota in the time it took to say the breed's name, but the person's perception of the dog has been altered dramatically.

American Pit Bull Terriers are highly energetic and love to run and play outdoors. Durable Nylabone® chew toys make playing more fun!

Having the ability to draw crowds with their extremely good sociable nature, American Pit Bull Terriers are excellent candidates for show competitions.

The breed, under various names and registries, has also excelled in the show ring. American Staffordshire Terriers are one of the few terriers to regularly take Group placements over the more traditional terrier types at American Kennel Club shows. In addition, both American Kennel Club American Staffordshire Terriers and United Kennel Club American Pit Bull Terriers often earn both conformation titles and obedience titles. Many owners believe that a well-balanced dog has titles at both ends of his registered name.

It is interesting to note that the American Pit Bull Terrier was the most decorated hero dog during World War I. "Stubby" was the war's most outstanding soldier. Not only did he earn the rank of sergeant, he also earned two medals.

Probably the most memorable American Pit Bull Terrier was "Pete," the canine star of *The Little Rascals* and *Our Gang* comedy series. His antics won the hearts of millions of viewers who could easily see his love and devotion for the children in both series.

The American Pit Bull Terrier also made the cover of *Life* magazine not once, but twice. Both times were in drawings by artist Will Rannells.

Not only have there been famous American Pit Bull Terriers throughout history but also a number of famous American Pit Bull Terrier owners. These include Theodore Roosevelt, Fred Astaire, James Caan, Jack Dempsey, Thomas Edison, Michael J. Fox, Helen Keller, Sir Walter Scott, and Jan Michael Vincent.

The American Pit Bull Terrier is loyal to his family members and will protect them at any cost.

SELECTING A PUPPY

Short-coated, sturdy breeds are much easier to evaluate as small puppies than their heavier-coated counterparts. It is easy to see exactly how the puppy is put together, his muscle development, and his movement.

The ideal American Pit Bull Terrier puppy is square in body with a prominent head and is somewhat cheeky in appearance, coupled with an outgoing, friendly disposition. The puppy should be self-assured, never shy, and well socialized with people and, if possible, children and other animals. He should be active, alert, and in high spirits. The joy of living you see in the puppy will survive his adolescence and continue well into adulthood. Long after his muzzle has turned gray and his eyesight has started to fail, there is still a zest for life that will keep dog and owner thinking and acting young.

Be careful not to let coat color unduly influence your choice. It is better to first select the best puppy as to structure and temperament that you possibly can and then consider the more cosmetic aspects of the breed.

However, before you make a final decision on the breed and/or a puppy, do your homework. No breed is perfect for everyone and the American Pit Bull Terrier may be too much dog for certain people. While this can be true of

Because of their short coats, the muscle development and movement of these American Pit Bull puppies can be easily seen.

Choosing an American Pit Bull puppy can be very difficult. These adorable puppies lounge in a comfortable bed of wood shavings.

every breed, it is more important when considering a breed like the American Pit Bull Terrier. Before you take your puppy home you need to realize that the public, including your neighbors, will most likely have a negative perception of the breed. You need to have not only a well-trained, well-socialized canine companion, but one that is exceptional in all ways. You also need to be prepared to intelligently discuss the breed without getting overly defensive.

Also, you should expect to be extensively questioned by the person from whom you want to buy a puppy. Due to reputation of the breed, breeders are very concerned about in whose hands they place their dogs. There are too many people out there who

Socializing your American Pit Bull puppy with neighbors, family members, and children will help accustom your dog to good social behavior.

The ideal American Pit Bull Terrier puppy is square in body with a prominent head and is somewhat cheeky in appearance.

Like all puppies, an American Pit Bull puppy needs lots of rest and will probably fall asleep from all the excitement of meeting his new family.

want a big, bad, macho dog to satisfy their own egos as well as those people who want to use the dogs for illegal or other undesirable purposes. Because of the breed's willingness to please and extreme loyalty to their owners, it is too easy to train them to inappropriately protect and attack. While it is the owner's fault and not that of the dog, it is best to prevent these situations from occurring in the first place, because the dog will almost always be the one who is blamed.

While no one wants to see a puppy he produced pass from one owner to another, it is interesting to note that American Pit Bull Terriers adjust extremely well to changes in ownership. They do not become excessively stressed in new environments and they will accept their new owners in a relatively short period of time. This is most likely due to their high degree of self confidence.

Puppies learn much from their parents or other older dogs. If you have an older American Pit Bull Terrier, he can be very helpful when training a new puppy.

BREED STANDARD

The American Pit Bull Terrier standard, as adopted by the United Kennel Club, is very broad and generalized. Thus, it is subject to a wide variety of interpretations, especially by others base their opinions almost solely on the head structure. If a good head is not present, it doesn't matter what other good points the dog possesses.

The American Pit Bull Terrier should be well-defined and thick-bodied but not over or underweight, which would throw off the dog's balance.

judges. The American Pit Bull Terrier is what is commonly known as a "head breed." While some judges and breeders want to see a total package as close to the ideal as described by the breed standard as possible,

UNITED KENNEL CLUB STANDARD FOR THE AMERICAN PIT BULL TERRIER

Head—Medium length. Bricklike in shape. Skull flat and widest at the ears, with prominent cheeks free from wrinkles.

Muzzle—Square, wide and deep. Well-pronounced jaws, displaying strength. Upper teeth should meet tightly over lower teeth, outside in front.

Ears—Cropped or uncropped (not important). Should be set high on head, and be free from wrinkles.

Eyes—Round. Should be set far apart, low down on the skull. Any color acceptable.

Nose—Wide-open nostrils. Any color acceptable.

Neck—Muscular. Slightly arched. Tapering from shoulder to head. Free from loose skin.

Shoulders—Strong and muscular, with wide sloping shoulder blades.

Back—Short and strong. Slightly sloping from withers to rump. Slightly arched at loins,

Although most breed standards are concerned with the total package of the dog, the American Pit Bull Terrier is considered a "head breed"—the head structure is most important.

which should be slightly tucked.

Chest—Deep, but not too broad, with wide sprung ribs.

Ribs—Close. Well sprung, with deep back ribs.

Tail—Short in comparison to

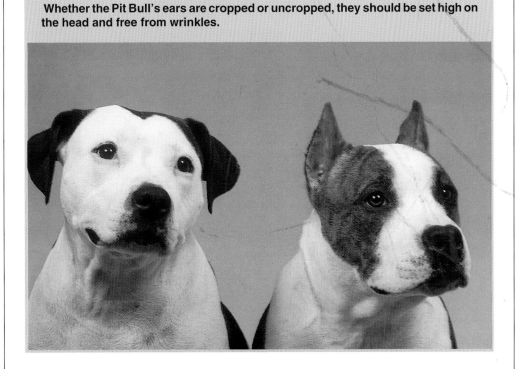

Whether the Pit Bull's ears are cropped or uncropped, they should be set high on the head and free from wrinkles.

size. Set low and tapering to a fine point. Not carried over back. Bobbed tail not acceptable.

Legs—Large, round boned, with straight, upright pasterns, reasonably strong. Feet to be of medium size. Gait should be light and springy. No rolling or pacing.

Thigh—Long with muscles developed. Hocks down and straight.

Coat—Glossy. Short and stiff to the touch.

Color—Any color or markings permissible.

Weight—Not important. Females preferred from 30 to 50 pounds. Males from 35 to 60 pounds.

The coat of the American Pit Bull Terrier is glossy, short, and stiff to the touch. This Pit Bull is being closely examined by a judge during competition.

SCALE OF POINTS

General appearance, personality and obedience	20
Head, muzzle, eyes, ears	25
Neck, shoulders and chest	15
Body	15
Legs and feet	15
Tail, coat and color	10
TOTAL	100

ANALYSIS OF THE STANDARD

The United Kennel Club standard for the American Pit Bull Terrier is one of the broadest, most generalized, and, therefore, most subjective standards in existence today. Even though there is a schedule of points included to show where the greater emphasis should be placed, it is usually used only where two or more specimens are extremely close to each other in conformation and the judge is finding it hard to decide between or amongst them. The various attributes of the breed are painted in bold strokes and very little, if any, guidance is given. Over the years, there have been several

The width and the depth of the American Pit Bull Terrier's head combine to produce a powerful image accentuated by well-developed cheeks and a strong jaw.

Proper alignment of teeth according to the American Pit Bull Terrier standard is a scissor bite, although other types of bite (level or pinchser and reverse scissor) still have the ability to catch and hold game.

attempts by fanciers and registries alike to get the American Pit Bull Terrier Club of America to propose a new, more detailed standard for the breed. However, with the stud book now open all year long for registration by inspection of dogs registered outside the United Kennel Club, there has been some reluctance to tighten the guidelines at this point in time. Thus, it is not surprising that the preferred judges are either breeder judges or ones coming from a similar type breed who can appreciate the dogs for what they are without the need of explanatory materials.

While some judges and breeders

want to see the American Pit Bull Terrier as a total functional package, there are many others that perceive it as a "head breed." That is, much more attention is paid to the head structure and appearance when judging the breed than is given to any other characteristic. While the American Pit Bull Terrier's head is extremely important when considering the origin of the dog as a fighting breed, or even from the perspective of a large game hunter, other features are also important and should be given equal consideration. After all, even the fighting dog had to have more than a strong, powerful jaw to engage in combat. He also needed to be quick and agile with the muscularity to take on an opponent. Unfortunately, the breed standard encourages the continuing "head breed" perception by assigning the greatest number of points to the features that compose the head.

Now let us consider the various components that make up the American Pit Bull Terrier, starting, of course, with the head.

The chest of the American Pit Bull Terrier is deep but not too broad. It provides the sufficient lung capacity needed for this active breed.

Natural ears on an American Pit Bull Terrier will usually stand semi-erect, folding at one-half to one-quarter up the ear leather. Cleaning the ears is very important because drop ears welcome bacteria that dwells in warm moist areas.

Head and Expression—The head should be broad and bricklike. The width and the depth of the head combine to produce a powerful image accentuated by well developed cheeks and a strong jaw. Recent years have seen a substantial decline in the cheekiness and underjaw of the breed to the point that many specimens are lacking in distinctive breed type.

The head, like the rest of the body, should appear balanced. No excessive skin or wrinkling should be apparent. The preferred "blockiness" is finely chiseled for expression. This lends a distinctive mobility to the face that can, at times, be comical.

Eyes—The wide-set eyes give the breed a bold, self confident expression that can be intimidating to those not familiar

Although the cropping of ears has been banned in most European countries, it is still allowed in the United States. People who prefer cropping say that it "cleans up the head," while others feel that it is unnecessary cosmetic surgery.

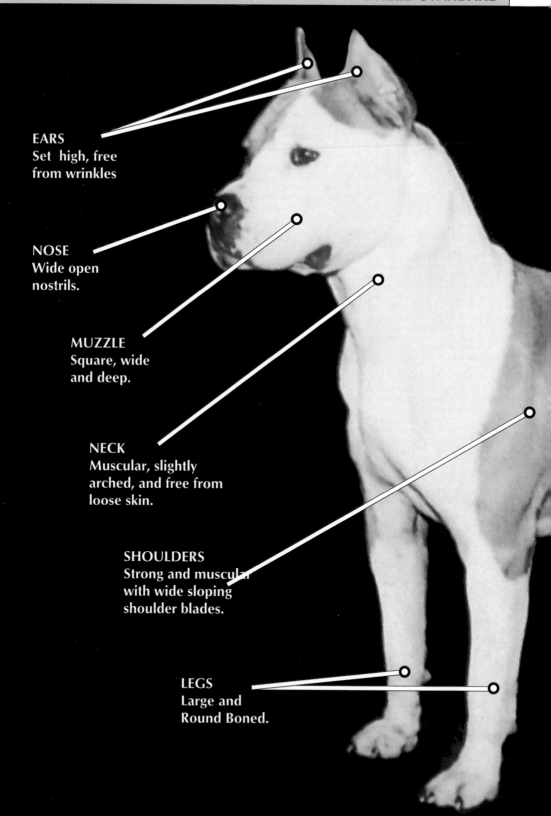

EARS
Set high, free
from wrinkles

NOSE
Wide open
nostrils.

MUZZLE
Square, wide
and deep.

NECK
Muscular, slightly
arched, and free from
loose skin.

SHOULDERS
Strong and muscular
with wide sloping
shoulder blades.

LEGS
Large and
Round Boned.

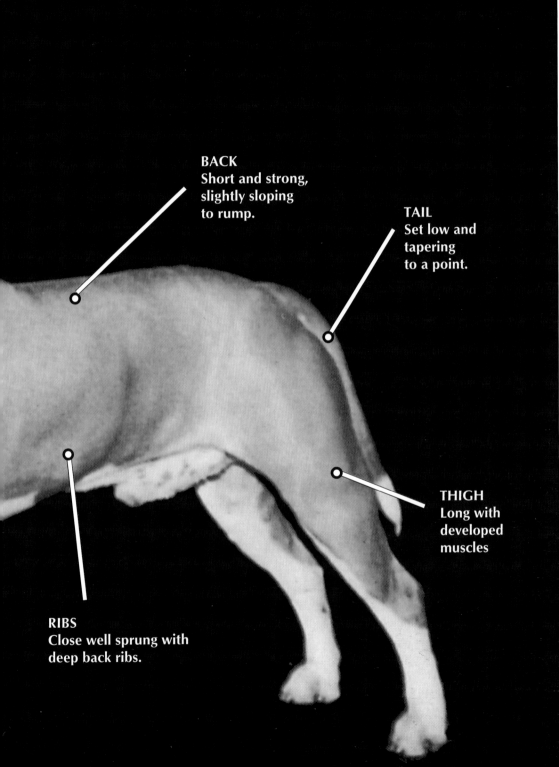

BACK
Short and strong,
slightly sloping
to rump.

TAIL
Set low and
tapering
to a point.

THIGH
Long with
developed
muscles

RIBS
Close well sprung with
deep back ribs.

According to the United Kennel Club standard, the American Pit Bull Terrier should move cleanly and effortlessly. This Pit Bull trots along poolside.

with the breed. American Pit Bull Terriers will usually meet their owner's and often a judge's eyes, further indicating their more than usual dominant character. While the United Kennel Club standard allows eyes of any color, those with lighter eyes, leaning toward the yellow "bird of prey" eye, which is unacceptable in most breeds, can have a cold threatening look that is often intimidating to the public.

Ears—The United Kennel Club standard allows cropped or uncropped ears, stating that it is not important. While the cropping of ears has been banned in most European countries, it is still allowed in most of the United States. Even though many veterinarians no longer crop ears, the procedure is still readily available for those who prefer that look. It is said that the cropping of the ears "cleans up the head." In fact, many judges have a difficult time putting up, or placing, an uncropped dog. Those who have done so are usually seen raising the dog's ears to the top of the head to see what it would look like if the ears had been cropped. At this point, it is whatever the viewer is used to looking at rather than the actual change in appearance that matters. Those used to looking at normally cropped breeds with natural ears have no problem with the look of the natural ears, while those used to seeing cropped ears on certain breeds find the natural ears offensive. It would not be surprising to see the United States follow suit and ban ear cropping sometime in the future given the reluctance of veterinarians to perform the procedure and the attitude of the general public against what they perceive as unnecessary cosmetic surgery. From another perspective, dispensing with ear cropping may impart a softer look to the breed and help in negating the public's perceived fear. However, many will argue that ear cropping is still functionally related in dogs that are hunting and herding. Another argument is that a cropped ear is healthier than a drop ear that closes over the ear canal and prevents adequate airflow as well as creates a dark, moist place where bacteria can flourish.

On the American Pit Bull Terrier, a cropped ear will be small and stand firmly erect. A natural ear will usually stand semi-erect, folding at one-half to one-quarter up the ear leather. A few will fold back into what is known as a rose ear.

Nose—Any color is allowed, though black is seen most often. Some variations do occur in certain coat colors, such as the self-color reds and the blues where the nose leather will accommodate itself to the coat color. Hence the term "red nose," which applies to certain individuals in the breed and sometimes particular kennels that are known for these colors and variations in pigmentation.

Bite—It is interesting that little is said about the jaw and

The American Pit Bull Terrier comes in a number of color varieties. In conformation competition, color is irrelevant in this breed, although white or primarily white dogs are usually frowned upon.

the bite in the United Kennel Club Standard. The jaw must be strong. The teeth should meet in a scissor bite, which is the strongest type of bite—it is considered ideal. However, there are slightly imperfect bites that can still do the job. A level or pinscher bite and a reverse scissor would still have the ability to catch and hold. These bite defects are more of a malocclusion of the teeth than the jaw. They would be considered cosmetic defects rather than functional problems. Definite over- and under-shot mouths would have more difficulty because often the jaws are also out of alignment, not just the teeth.

Neck and Shoulders— After the head, the development and placement of the neck and shoulders is another important breed characteristic. The well-developed musculature not only adds power to the dog but also accentuates the arch of the neck and offsets the depth and breadth of chest that provides the sufficient lung capacity for this active canine. The hindquarters are also extremely well muscled to balance out the forequarters and the head.

Back—The back is short and strong, giving the American Pit Bull Terrier a square appearance. As with most smooth-coated breeds with squarish frames, the eye should travel smoothly from the nose to the rump without stopping. If one feature along the way causes the eye to hesitate, it is usually incorrect. This is true of both sexes even though the females may be slightly longer in the back than the males.

Weight and Height—Here is where weight, though not considered important in the standard, plays a crucial role in the appearance of the breed. It only takes five pounds over or under to throw off the balance of an American Pit Bull Terrier. An overweight dog will have little tuck up at the loin and look like a stuffed sausage. A dog that is underweight will appear too refined and light, even with well-developed muscles. Until you develop an eye for the weight of your dog, a good guide is that you should be able to feel, but not see, the ribs.

Height, which is not

Razors Edge Throwin Knuckles, owned by David Wilson, is a well-built Pit Bull. His deep chest and powerful legs are characteristic of the breed.

mentioned in the United Kennel Club standard, also affects the overall balance of the breed. As an indicator, the American Staffordshire Terrier standard states about size, "Height and weight should be in proportion. A height of about 18 to 19 inches at the shoulders for the male and 17 to 18 inches for the female is to be considered preferable." This is not to say that dogs above and below these guidelines are incorrect, but that the most perfectly balanced specimens of the breed appear most often around these heights. There may be large dogs that are perfectly proportioned, but they will be the exception rather than the rule.

Legs—The legs are large and strongly boned in order to support the bulk and weight of the dog. The front legs are straight while the rear legs are moderately angulated. Be aware that some lines have a recurring problem known commonly as "popping hocks." More properly referred to as luxating patellae, the ball will literally pop out of the joint structure in which it sits. This means that either the ball is malformed or the cuff in which it sits is too shallow. While this can be seen if it occurs during movement, it is relatively easy to test for by applying slight pressure on the involved rear joint. Movement can be felt, and even sometimes heard.

Gait—A properly structured dog should be able to move cleanly and effortlessly. American Pit Bull Terriers should give the impression of boldness and confidence as they easily cover ground. Their backs should remain level, without any indication of rolling, once they are mature. Their movement is typical of the terrier breeds in that they double track rather than single track. The legs will tend not to move toward the center line of the body when at a trot. Puppies and young adolescents may still show a slight looseness when moving and should not be penalized for lack of age and development.

Coat—A healthy dog will have a coat that literally glows. Color is irrelevant, but some judges have a dislike for white or primarily white dogs.

When viewed from the front, the American Pit Bull's legs should be straight and strongly built in order to support the bulky weight of the dog.

FEEDING YOUR PIT BULL

Now let's talk about feeding your Pit Bull, a subject so simple that it's amazing there is so much nonsense and misunderstanding about it. Is it expensive to feed a Pit Bull? No, it is not! You can feed your Pit Bull economically and keep him in perfect shape the year round, or you can feed him

dogs flatly refuse to eat nice, fresh beef. They pick around it and eat everything else. But meat—bah! Why? They aren't accustomed to it! They'd eat rabbit fast enough, but they refuse beef because they aren't used to it.

Variety in diet is not necessary for American Pit Bull Terriers. Buy a nutritious dog food and stick with it day in and day out.

year round, or you can feed him expensively. He'll thrive either way, and let's see why this is true.

First of all, remember a Pit Bull is a dog. Dogs do not have a high degree of selectivity in their food, and unless you spoil them with great variety (and possibly turn them into poor, "picky" eaters) they will eat almost anything that they become accustomed to. Many

VARIETY NOT NECESSARY

A good general rule of thumb is forget all human preferences and don't give a thought to variety. Choose the right diet for your Pit Bull and feed it to him day after day, year after year, winter and summer. But what is the right diet?

Hundreds of thousands of dollars have been spent in canine

Fresh clean water should be available to your dog at all times. This is important for good health throughout his lifetime.

satisfactory, and easily available in stores everywhere in containers of five to 50 pounds. Larger amounts cost less per pound, usually.

If you have a choice of brands, it is usually safer to choose the better known one; but even so, carefully read the analysis on the package. Do not choose any food in which the protein level is less than 25 percent, and be sure that this protein comes from both animal and vegetable sources. The good dog foods have meat meal, fish meal, liver, and such, plus protein from alfalfa and soy beans, as well as some dried-milk

Occasionally giving your American Pit Bull the vitamin C found in most fruits is a good supplement. Avoid vitamin D, however, and don't supplement unless directed by a veterinarian.

nutrition research. The results are pretty conclusive, so you needn't go into a lot of experimenting with trials of this and that every other week. Research has proven just what your dog needs to eat and to keep healthy.

DOG FOOD

There are almost as many right diets as there are dog experts, but the basic diet most often recommended is one that consists of a dry food, either meal or kibble form. There are several of excellent quality, manufactured by reliable companies, research tested, and nationally advertised. They are inexpensive, highly product. Note the vitamin content carefully. See that they are all there in good proportions; and be especially certain that the food contains properly high levels of vitamins A and D, two of the most perishable and important ones. Note the B-complex level, but don't worry about carbohydrate and mineral levels. These substances are plentiful and cheap and not likely to be lacking in a good brand.

The advice given for how to choose a dry food also applies to moist or canned types of dog foods, if you decide to feed one of these.

Having chosen a really good food, feed it to your Pit Bull as the manufacturer directs. And once you've started, stick to it. Never change if you can possibly help it. A switch from one meal or kibble-type food can usually be made without too much upset; however, a change will almost invariably give you (and your Pit Bull) some trouble.

WHEN SUPPLEMENTS ARE NEEDED

Now what about supplements of various kinds, mineral and vitamin, or the various oils? They are all okay to add to your Pit Bull's food. However, if you are feeding your Pit Bull a correct diet, and this is easy to do, no supplements are necessary unless your Pit Bull has been improperly fed, has been sick, or is having puppies. Vitamins and minerals are naturally present in all the foods; and to ensure against any loss through processing, they are added in concentrated form to the dog food you use. Except on the advice of your veterinarian, added amounts of vitamins can prove harmful to your Pit Bull! The same risk goes with minerals.

FEEDING SCHEDULE

When and how much food to

Exercise is important for your Pit Bull's good health, and so are safe toys for him to play with. The Nylabone® Wishbone® is a durable toy with an interesting shape.

Giving your American Pit Bull a Nylabone® does three important things: cleans his teeth, provides safe chewing pleasure, and keeps your dog happy!

chew on while their teeth and jaws are developing—for cutting the puppy teeth, to induce growth of the permanent teeth under the puppy teeth, to assist in getting rid of the puppy teeth at the proper time, to help the permanent teeth through the gums, to ensure normal jaw development, and to settle the permanent teeth solidly in the jaws.

The adult Pit Bull's desire to chew stems from the instinct for tooth cleaning, gum massage, and jaw exercise—plus the need for an outlet for periodic doggie tensions.

Even though your Pit Bull may not believe you, Nylafloss® is not a toy but a most effective agent in controlling plaque.

give your Pit Bull? Most dogs do better if fed two or three smaller meals per day—this is not only better but vital to larger and deep-chested dogs. As to how to prepare the food and how much to give, it is generally best to follow the directions on the food package. Your own Pit Bull may want a little more or a little less.

Fresh, cool water should always be available to your Pit Bull. This is important to good health throughout his lifetime.

ALL PIT BULLS NEED TO CHEW

Puppies and young Pit Bulls need something with resistance to

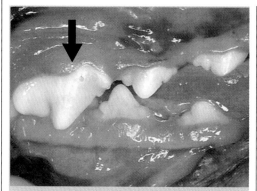

This scientific study shows a dog's teeth while being maintained by Nylabone® chewing.

This is why dogs, especially puppies and young dogs, will often destroy property worth hundreds of dollars when their chewing instinct is not diverted

Feeding your Pit Bull a nutritious dog food will keep him in top condition. Some types of dog food, especially dry food, help to clean your dog's teeth as he eats.

from their owner's possessions. And this is why you should provide your Pit Bull with something to chew—something that has the necessary functional qualities, is desirable from the Pit Bull's viewpoint, and is safe for him.

It is very important that your Pit Bull not be permitted to chew on anything he can break or on any indigestible thing from which he can bite sizable chunks. Sharp pieces, such as from a bone which can be broken by a dog, may

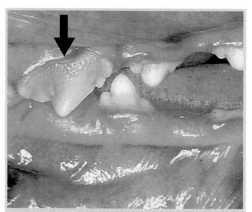

The Nylabone® was taken away, and in 30 days the teeth were almost completely covered with plaque and tartar.

pierce the intestinal wall and kill. Indigestible things that can be bitten off in chunks, such as from shoes or rubber or plastic toys, may cause an intestinal stoppage (if not regurgitated) and bring painful death, unless surgery is promptly performed.

Strong natural bones, such as 4- to 8-inch lengths of round shin bone from mature beef—either the kind you can get from a butcher or one of the variety available commercially in pet stores—may serve your Pit Bull's teething

When you say jump, your American Pit Bull Terrier will jump as high as he can to get a hold of a Nylabone®.

The durable Nylabone® FRISBEE disc with the bone molded on top will give you and your American Pit Bull plenty of enjoyment—just make sure he gives back!

needs if his mouth is large enough to handle them effectively. You may be tempted to give your Pit Bull puppy a smaller bone and he may not be able to break it when you do, but puppies grow rapidly and the power of their jaws constantly increases until maturity. This means that a growing Pit Bull may break one of the smaller bones at any time, swallow the pieces, and die painfully before you realize what is wrong.

All hard natural bones are very abrasive. If your Pit Bull is an avid chewer, natural bones may wear away his teeth prematurely; hence, they then should be taken away from your dog when the teething purposes have been served. The badly worn, and usually painful, teeth of many mature dogs can be traced to excessive chewing on natural bones.

Contrary to popular belief,

Chewing helps to keep your Pit Bull Terrier's teeth clean. By providing your dog with safe chew toys, such as those made by Nylabone®, you can prevent him from chewing things that may be harmful.

Feeding your Pit Bull Terrier immediately before or after he exercises can be unhealthy for him. Allowing your dog to digest his meal prior to exercising and to rest after play periods will prevent digestive problems.

knuckle bones that can be chewed up and swallowed by your Pit Bull provide little, if any, usable calcium or other nutriment. They do, however, disturb the digestion of most dogs and cause them to vomit the nourishing food they need.

Dried rawhide products of various types, shapes, sizes, and prices are available on the market and have become quite popular. However, they don't serve the primary chewing functions very well; they are a bit messy when wet from mouthing, and most Pit Bulls chew them up rather rapidly—but they have been considered safe for dogs until recently. Now, more and more incidents of death, and near death, by strangulation have been reported to be the results of partially swallowed chunks of rawhide swelling in the throat. More recently, some veterinarians have been attributing cases of acute constipation to large pieces of incompletely digested rawhide in the intestine.

A new product, molded rawhide, is very safe. During the process, the rawhide is melted and then injection molded into the familiar dog shape. It is very hard and is eagerly accepted by

Nylabones® come in many different shapes, sizes, and colors. Your Pit Bull will love his Nylabone® and take it with him everywhere.

Your Pit Bull will be your best friend if you take care of him properly.

Pit Bulls. The melting process also sterilizes the rawhide. Don't confuse this with pressed rawhide, which is nothing more than small strips of rawhide squeezed together.

The nylon bones, especially those with natural meat and bone fractions added, are probably the most complete, safe, and economical answer to the chewing need. Dogs cannot break them or bite off sizable chunks; hence, they are completely safe—and being longer lasting than other things offered for the purpose, they are economical.

Hard chewing raises little bristle-like projections on the surface of the nylon bones—to provide effective interim tooth cleaning and vigorous gum massage, much in the same way

If you are leaving your Pit Bull Terrier unattended while you are away for the day, make sure you provide him with plenty of food and water. Supplying him with some Nylabone® chew toys will also help keep him out of trouble.

your toothbrush does it for you. The little projections are raked off and swallowed in the form of thin shavings, but the chemistry of the nylon is such that they break down in the stomach fluids and pass through without effect.

The toughness of the nylon provides the strong chewing resistance needed for important jaw exercise and effectively aids teething functions, but there is no tooth wear because nylon is non-abrasive. Being inert, nylon does not support the growth of

There are so many good Nylabone® products, from colorful bones to durable flying discs, that your American Pit Bull Terrier will have a hard time deciding what to chew on first.

microorganisms; and it can be washed in soap and water or it can be sterilized by boiling or in an autoclave.

Nylabone® is highly recommended by veterinarians as a safe, healthy nylon bone that can't splinter or chip. Nylabone® is frizzled by the dog's chewing action, creating a toothbrush-like surface that cleanses the teeth and massages the gums. Nylabone®, the only chew products made of flavor-impregnated solid nylon, are available in your local pet shop. Nylabone® is superior to the cheaper bones because it is made of virgin nylon, which is the strongest and longest-lasting type of nylon available. The cheaper bones are made from recycled or re-ground nylon scraps, and have a tendency to break apart and split easily.

Nothing, however, substitutes for periodic professional attention for your Pit Bull's teeth and gums, not any more than your toothbrush can do that for you. Have your Pit Bull's teeth cleaned at least once a year by your veterinarian (twice a year is better) and he will be happier, healthier, and far more pleasant to live with.

Your Pit Bull Terrier pup will require a different type of dog food than your adult dog. Check with your veterinarian or breeder for recommendations on which food is right for your dog.

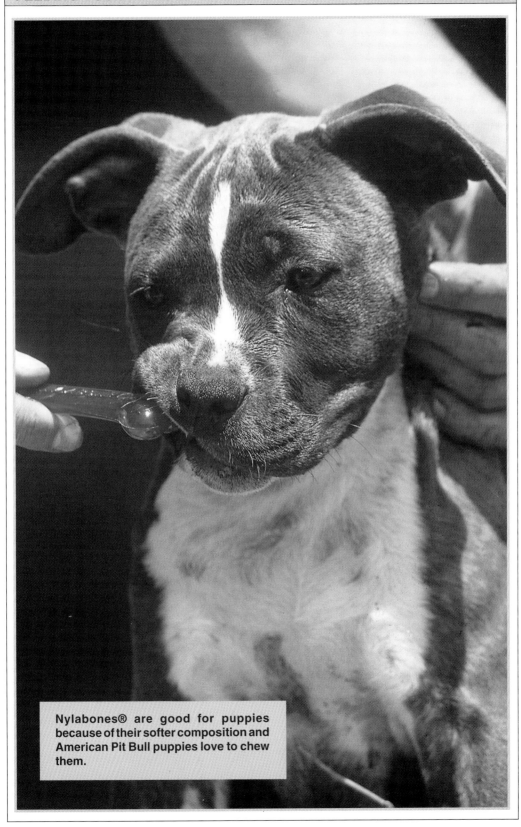

Nylabones® are good for puppies because of their softer composition and American Pit Bull puppies love to chew them.

GROOMING YOUR PIT BULL

The American Pit Bull Terrier has a close, single coat that requires minimal care and maintenance. A weekly brushing to keep shedding to a minimum and an occasional bath should

nail trimming routine and keep up with it from the first week you bring your puppy home, and you should never have a problem. Many dogs do not like to have their feet handled and it is much

As good as American Pit Bull Terriers are at cleaning themselves and their puppies, they still need help from their masters sometimes. Keeping your dog clean is important to his health.

take care of the dog's coat quite nicely. However, you may want to look into the color enhancing shampoos on the market if you intend to show your dog.

Careful attention should be paid to the nails. Nails should be kept very short in order to keep the feet neat and tight. A grinder is the best method of keeping the nails as short as possible. Start a

easier to struggle with an eight-week-old puppy than a well-muscled adult.

If your puppy comes home with newly cropped ears, you will need to provide the after care while they heal and, possibly, some minimal taping to make them stand properly. While the ears are still stitched and healing, apply a medicated powder that can be

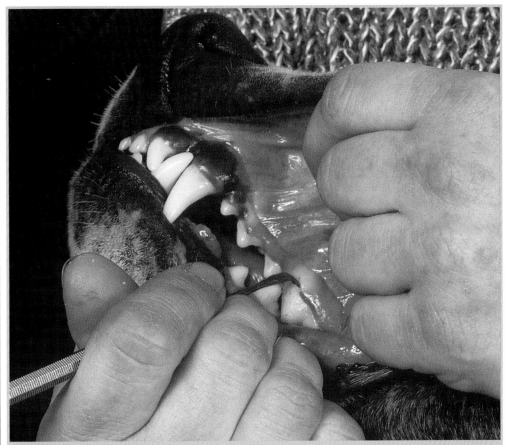

Scaling and cleaning a dog's teeth is one method of preventing tartar accumulation. Additionally, owners need to provide the dog with hard chew bones, such as Nylabone® products.

found in most drug stores. It should be used for at least four or five days on the cut edges of the ears. This will promote healing and relieve the itchiness that may cause the puppy to scratch and pull out the stitches. Once the ears have scabbed over, begin using aloe vera cream with natural vitamin E. After the stitches have been removed or have completely dissolved, start massaging the ears upward into the position in which you want them to stand. Warm olive oil, an ointment, or nothing at all can be used during the massage. This helps keep the cut edges stretched during the final healing process while making the ears stand more quickly.

When cropped, the American Pit Bull Terrier's ears are cut very short and will often stand on their own. However, if they flop outward toward the side of the head or pull toward the top of the head, some minor intervention will be necessary if they are to stand correctly. First, make sure that the cut edge of the ear is completely healed and that all stitches have either dissolved or been removed. If the ear is flopping outward, pull the ear upright, really stretching it, and tape with the natural fold of the ear. The fold is present on the inside uncut edge of the ear. Thus, if you are facing the dog, the ear on your left will be taped from left to right while the ear on your right will be taped from right to left. Start the tape at the base of the ear and wrap it around the ear in an upward spiral until it appears as a slight cone on either side of the skull. If the ears are pulling inward, you would tape in the opposite direction. Unfold the natural fold of the ear and tape against it in order to reverse the cartilage into its proper position. If you are facing the dog, the ear to your left will be taped from right to left and the ear on your right will be taped from left to right. Leave the ears taped for about five days. If retaping is

Being meticulous about your Pit Bull's cleanliness is sure to help keep him disease free, parasite free, and dirt free.

Your Pit Bull's nails should be kept very short in order to keep the feet neat and tight. Clipping regularly will prevent nail overgrowth problems.

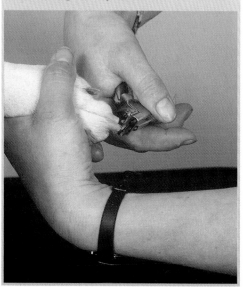

necessary, let the ears breathe for two to three days before retaping.

There is a no-tape method using mole skin and skin bond that works well in some breeds, but the American Pit Bull Terrier's ears are short and the mole skin does not work as well as it does on thc longer ears of a Boxer, Doberman, or Great Dane.

A clean American Pit Bull Terrier is a joy to have!

TRAINING YOUR PIT BULL

You owe proper training to your Pit Bull. The right and privilege of being trained is his birthright; and whether your Pit Bull is going to be a handsome, well-mannered housedog and companion, a show dog, or whatever possible use he may be put to, the basic training is always the same—all must start with basic obedience, or what might be called "manner training."

Your Pit Bull must come instantly when called and obey the "Sit" or "Down" command just as fast; he must walk quietly at "Heel," whether on or off lead. He must be mannerly and polite wherever he goes; he must be polite to strangers on the street and in stores. He must be mannerly in the presence of other dogs. He must not bark at

Teaching your American Pit Bull Terrier to stay in the down position requires keeping your foot on the lead and stepping backward.

American Pit Bulls are very expressive in their body language. When they are happy to see you, they will often jump up to hug you.

Training your Pit Bull to jump obstacles takes time, patience, and a little help from you. This trainer uses a leash to help the dog learn.

Teaching your dog to sit is one of the most important and basic lessons you should teach your dog. It is a simple command that should be relatively easy to teach.

children on roller skates, motorcycles, or other domestic animals. And he must be restrained from chasing cats. It is not a dog's inalienable right to chase cats, and he must be reprimanded for it.

The American Pit Bull Terrier is highly intelligent and willing to try anything and everything you want him to learn. However, that keen intelligence, high energy level, and innate enthusiasm will often get in the way of what you are trying to accomplish.

Overall, the new owner will find his American Pit Bull Terrier to be relatively easy to train and tractable in most situations, even around other dogs.

The earlier you start working with your American Pit Bull

In more advanced stages of training, you can train your American Pit Bull with hand signals. This is quite difficult, so you should be proud of your accomplishments!

Terrier, the better. It is highly recommended that you find a local Kindergarten Puppy Training (KPT) class in your area, which will usually accept puppies as early as 12 weeks. The class consists of very light, basic obedience training with plenty of play and praise. You and your puppy will learn the basics of what makes a polite dog, and your puppy will start bonding closer and working better with you as well as socializing with other young dogs. Later classes will work to reinforce and expand what you have already learned.

American Pit Bull Terriers require a firm but loving hand. They are willing to please and they learn quickly, but they can become bored easily. Variety is the key to their activity. They are sensitive to your tone of voice and want more than anything to please you. The more you encourage and praise the American Pit Bull Terrier, the more responsive he will be to your commands as you work to the point where you and your dog function as a team. Once you reach that point, the world of dog activities is wide open to you and your American Pit Bull Terrier.

Remember that the American Pit Bull Terrier is highly expressive both in facial features and body language. He will show his delight in meeting a friend with much tail wagging and body bouncing. He will demonstrate interest by cocking his head and furrowing his brow. He will sometimes show displeasure or hurt feelings by turning his back to you or refusing to look you in the face. His expressions are relatively easy to read and every owner should pay attention to what his dog's body language is attempting to convey.

The American Pit Bull Terrier is a naturally muscular breed and does not need to be road worked or excessively exercised to develop his appropriate musculature. While weight pulling and other related activities will enhance his strength, they are not needed for his physical development. However, the activities are fun and you and your American Pit Bull Terrier may enjoy trying them out together.

Also consider those activities that place the dog in the most positive light. In addition to obedience, owners should consider obtaining a Canine Good Citizen certificate on each and every dog they own. Some municipalities have agreed to accept these certificates as proof that the dog has a good temperament and is well trained.

Another related activity is that of a therapy dog. These are dogs that are tested and certified to visit health care facilities, educational institutions, and the like. Owners who have trained and certified their dogs and who regularly take their dogs out in public have done wonders for the perception of the breed.

Finally, do not wait until someone sees your dog and panics. Take the initiative and introduce him to the neighbors, local officials, and anyone else who will listen. Show them that you have a friendly, well-trained, and well-socialized animal that is not something to fear.

PROFESSIONAL TRAINING

How do you go about this training? Well, it's a very simple procedure, pretty well standardized by now. First, if you can afford the extra expense, you may send your Pit Bull to a professional trainer, where in 30 to 60 days he will learn how to be a "good dog." If you enlist the services of a good professional trainer, follow his advice of when to come to see the dog. No, he won't forget you, but too-frequent visits at the wrong time may slow down his training progress. And

In open obedience trials, the dog, starting from the heel position, must retrieve a "dumbbell" thrown by the owner. American Pit Bull Terriers are good utility dogs and can perform this function as well as any dog.

using a "pro" trainer means that you will have to go for some training, too, after the trainer feels your Pit Bull is ready to go home. You will have to learn how your Pit Bull works, just what to expect of him and how to use what the dog has learned after he is home.

OBEDIENCE TRAINING CLASS

Another way to train your Pit Bull (many experienced Pit Bull suggestions to you and also tell you when and how to correct your Pit Bull's errors. Then, too, working with such a group, your Pit Bull will learn to get along with other dogs. And, what is more important, he will learn to do exactly what he is told to do, no matter how much confusion there is around him or how great the temptation is to go his own way.

Write to your national kennel club for the location of a training

Although the American Pit Bull is not commonly thought of as a showdog, many Pit Bulls and their owners have become involved in conformation and other areas of the dog sport.

people think this is the best) is to join an obedience training class right in your own community. There is such a group in nearly every community nowadays. Here you will be working with a group of people who are also just starting out. You will actually be training your own dog, since all work is done under the direction of a head trainer who will make club or class in your locality. Sign up. Go to it regularly—every session! Go early and leave late! Both you and your Pit Bull will benefit tremendously.

TRAIN HIM BY THE BOOK

The third way of training your Pit Bull is by the book. Yes, you can do it this way and do a good job of it too. But in using the book method, select a book, buy it, study it carefully; then study it some more, until the procedures are almost second nature to you. Then start your training. But stay with the book and its advice and exercises. Don't start in and then make up a few rules of your own.

American Pit Bull Terriers love the springpole, and it helps them get plenty of exercise.

Lots of love and attention will help your new Pit Bull Terrier during training sessions. Praise him for following a command with a treat, a new chew toy, or simply a hug.

If you don't follow the book, you'll get into jams you can't get out of by yourself. If after a few hours of short training sessions your Pit Bull is still not working as he should, get back to the book for a study session, because it's your fault, not the dog's! The procedures of dog training have been so well systemized that it must be your fault, since literally thousands of fine Pit Bulls have been trained by the book.

After your Pit Bull is "letter perfect" under all conditions, then, if you wish, go on to advanced training and trick work.

Your Pit Bull will love his obedience training, and you'll burst with pride at the finished product! Your Pit Bull will enjoy life even more, and you'll enjoy your Pit Bull more. And remember—you *owe good training to your Pit Bull.*

A heavy lead and collar are very important when training a strong dog like the American Pit Bull Terrier.

REGISTERING AND SHOWING

REGISTRATION

Even though the American Pit Bull Terrier was the first breed registered by the United Kennel Club, not all registered specimens of the breed carry the distinguished "Purple Ribbon" or "PR" pedigree since not all

(e.g., the American Dog Breeders Association or the American Kennel Club). Today, the stud books stay open all year long and many dogs are the first of their lines to be registered with the United Kennel Club.

For each dog, the United Kennel

If you are willing to put in the same time, study, and keen observation as a professional handler, you can learn how to show your own dog.

registrants have full United Kennel Club registration behind them. Previously, the American Pit Bull Terrier Club of America had allowed the United Kennel Club's stud books to be opened for three months each year for registration by inspection to bring in acceptable dogs of the breed that were registered elsewhere

Club issues a registration certificate and a three-generation pedigree. Both of these documents are necessary in order to enter a show licensed by the United Kennel Club. However, you may obtain a "Quick Entry Card" to make things easier.

A rather interesting aspect of the United Kennel Club's

registration system is their policy concerning the inbreeding of dogs. When a breeder submits a litter application that is inbred, the United Kennel Club issues the puppy slips marked "inbred." While some feel that this is an indication of their displeasure with the whole concept of inbreeding, that is not the case. Rather, they believe that anyone sufficiently knowledgeable to inbreed should be able to explain and justify what they did. If you cannot explain it, you should not have done it in the first place.

Inbreeding should only be attempted by those with sufficient experience to honestly evaluate the two dogs involved as well as the resulting litter. Dogs that are to be inbred must be exceptional specimens of the breed. The litter has the potential to produce the best of the best and the worst of the worst. Those who inbreed usually enter into it with the attitude that if they get one superb puppy, the risk was worth it. Also, once you inbreed, the resulting puppies must be outcrossed. Repeated inbreeding will ultimately reduce size,

The American Pit Bull Terrier is a handsome, intelligent dog that is full of expression and life.

substance, and intelligence as well as exacerbate existing genetic problems.

SHOWING

If you have ever shown at American Kennel Club conformation shows and want to start showing at United Kennel Club shows, forget everything you have ever learned.

Each breed recognized by the United Kennel Club shows independently of any other breed. While a club may host a multi-breed show and offer competition beyond the breed level, these are fun classes only and do not carry championship points. Class dogs, those working towards championship titles, compete against each other through Best in Show for points that are assigned to each win. Classes are divided by age so that puppies compete against puppies, adolescents against adolescents, and mature dogs against mature dogs. A total of 100 points, which must include at least one "major," is required for a championship title. A major is a Best Male or Best Female in Show. A dog may earn up to 35 points at any given show. Points may be awarded even though a dog never beats another of its breed because points are assigned on a per win basis rather than on the number of dogs defeated.

Champions of record never compete against class dogs. The Champion of Champions class wins accumulate toward the three required for a Grand Championship title. Beyond that there are only fun classes for qualification into invitationals throughout the year. Professional handlers are not allowed. However, someone else may show your dog with your written permission, but not for a fee. No baiting is allowed, though you may stack the dog and talk to him in the ring.

The United Kennel Club shows are usually very relaxed and friendly. There has been a concerted effort to keep the politics out of the shows, but those who are highly competitive will find them somewhat limited. Also, the minimal number of shows that are held will require extensive travel if you want to finish a dog in a relatively short time.

Obedience is another type of

The American Pit Bull is known for his strong jaws and teeth. A handler show his Pit Bull's teeth to the judge for examination.

These two American Pit Bull Terriers await their turn in the show ring.

showing which has become quite popular. The United Kennel Club obedience trials also differ from their American Kennel Club counterparts, but not as dramatically as the conformation events. One of the major differences is that the novice competition includes jumps. However, the height is more reasonable, which has gained the support of many obedience exhibitors.

POLICY ON FIGHTING DOGS

During the height of the media craze regarding "pit bulls," the United Kennel Club, the American Kennel Club, and the American Dog Owners Association presented a united front to protect their respective breeds as well as the rights of dogdom in general.

The United Kennel Club propagated and repeatedly published a strong policy with penalties for individuals and clubs found to be involved in any way with the fighting of American Pit Bull Terriers. This notice was also required to be published in all show information that was made available to the public. Penalties included the revocation of registrations and registration privileges.

YOUR PIT BULL'S HEALTH

The American Pit Bull Terrier is a relatively healthy breed with few genetic health problems. This is most likely due to the origin of the breed for bull and bear baiting as well as dog fighting. The name of the game was survival, and only the best and strongest would make the cut and ultimately be bred. Thus there were few of the commonly known defects bred into the early specimens of the breed. This remained true during their early history in America because of their highly functional uses in sport and other working capacities. However, later generations did not have the advantages of the natural selection process and as puppies that would not normally have survived were saved by breeders, a variety of ills began to surface.

As a medium-sized breed, as opposed to a large breed, there is some hip dysplasia and it is recommended that all breeding stock is x-rayed and certified

Some American Pit Bull Terriers have acute flea allergies where one flea bite can set off a generalized scratching and chewing of the coat and skin.

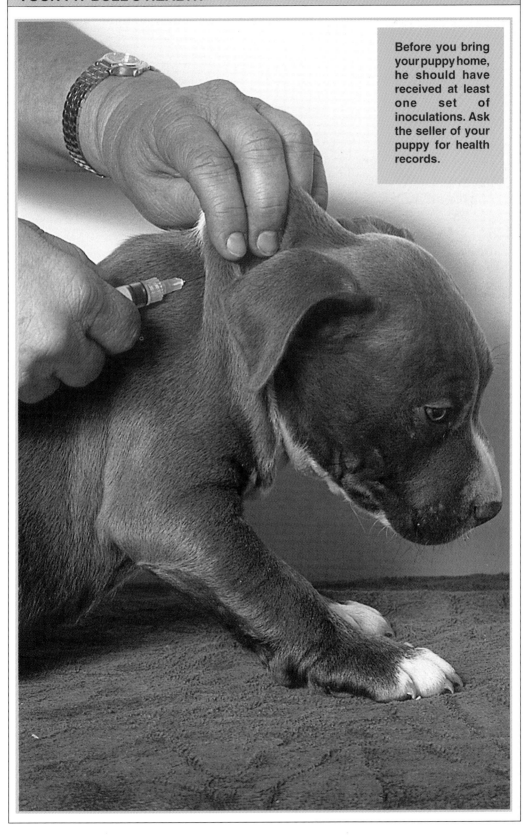

Before you bring your puppy home, he should have received at least one set of inoculations. Ask the seller of your puppy for health records.

The American Pit Bull Terrier, because it is a smooth-coated breed, is prone to forming calluses on the pressure points of the body. A soft bed is one way to help prevent these calluses from forming.

through either the Orthopedic Foundation for Animals (OFA) or the PennHip™ program sponsored by International Canine Genetics (ICG). The x-rays are important in this breed because American Pit Bull Terriers are insensitive to pain and may not show overt symptoms of the condition, leaving the average owner unaware that a problem exists before breeding the dog. Hip dysplasia is a polygenetic hereditary disorder and affected animals should not be bred.

Some American Pit Bull Terriers have skin sensitivities that occasionally result in demodectic or teenage mange that is readily treatable in the localized form. Others have flea allergies where only one bite is sufficient to set off a generalized scratching and chewing of the coat and skin.

The American Pit Bull Terrier, like most other smooth-coated, muscular breeds, will have a tendency to form calluses on the pressure points of his body. This will most often occur on the knees, elbows, hocks, and legs. The weight of the body, unprotected by fat and hair, will form its own protective barrier when it connects repeatedly with hard surfaces. A good way to prevent this is to keep the dog at a proper weight and to provide sufficient bedding between the dog and his sleeping surface. The application of a softening cream can also help in the event that a callus begins to form. However, it is better to keep the dog from developing calluses in the first place rather than trying to make them go away later.